# A Journey of Sorts

MEYER H. GOLDMAN

# A JOURNEY OF SORTS

poems by

## Meyer H. Goldman

edited by

## James L. Limbacher

illustrated by

James Stockham

HARLO                    DETROIT

Copyright © 1981 by Meyer H. Goldman

Printed by Harlo Press, 50 Victor, Detroit, Michigan 48203

For my children

# Foreword

First of all, let me say that I never met Meyer H. Goldman. Why, then, am I editing his book of poetry? The answer is merely that I was asked.

Meyer H. Goldman called me in 1976 to ask if the Henry Ford Centennial Library in Dearborn (where I was the audio-visual librarian) would like to have his record collection. He very honestly told me that he was dying and I somehow refused to believe it. Then the calls stopped and it was the Spring of 1979 when he called me again and said that he had arrested the disease for three years but that he was weakening and he wanted to be sure that his thoughts he had put on paper in the form of his poems would be published. He chose me because he had seen me on television and also because I had already edited 13 books of my own.

Mr. Goldman was beloved by many people and I soon began to realize what a beautiful person he was and how unfortunate I was not to have been able to know him personally. I began reading his poems, consulting with an artist to do the illustrations (James Stockham was an obvious choice, since I had known him and his work for 25 years and sensed that his superb talent would complement the poems perfectly) and generally getting the material ready for publication.

The material was ready in August of 1979 and I called Mr. Goldman's lawyer to inform him of this fact and to ask how Mr. Goldman was getting along. It was then that I was told that the man had died a few weeks before.

To this very day, I don't know what Meyer H. Goldman looks like and I have never met his children. But I know he must have loved them very much, as these poems will attest. I hope they, and you, appreciate the simplicity and sincerity of his poems — poems which conjure up the image of a man I can never forget. Through his poems I feel I know him very well.

I am honored to edit this volume in his memory.

—James L. Limbacher
January, 1981

# Contents

# Fragment

Dimly seen through the trees
cold stars like diamonds
glisten . . .
as they
listen . . .
listen . . .
to the wind go by . . .

# The Snow
# Came Today

The snow came today
quietly serenely peacefully
it arrived
unhurt
and not lacerated by
the wind
as i have known it
but
with a benign blessing
it came
softly softly
and
in hushed stillness
covered
the earth
for its winter sleep.

# Legacy

The blood will forget.
The mind will forget.

Things done and undone . . . things said and
    unsaid—
The snow . . . the rain . . . death . . .
God.

The blood *will* forget.
The mind *will* forget.

But the heart remembers.
The heart remembers.

# Streetcorner
# in March

In the night
the city is still

caught between
life and death
undecided
the city is silent

it lies bleak
      naked
      cold

nothing moves
along the street
but
      the wind
      shadows
      yesterday's newspaper . . .

## Author

From seed . . . a tree.
How kind
A deed
To leave such signature
For me.

# Eternal

The earth revolves . . .
The season changes . . .
The snow forms
Grimy rivulets
And life reappears
When there was none . . .
The world
Awakens . . .
New.

# Two Quatrains

I
Rosebuds blinking in the sun
Open petals one by one;
Ten thousand winds blew in vain
To do the work of drops of rain.

II
Teardrops flow without a sound,
Always lost yet never found;
A teardrop's flow is to me
The most profound of mystery.

# Treasure

Plucked from sand
In moonlit night,
Poised on hand
As though for flight . . .
A sea shell,
Pink and white.

Angel's horn
To rouse the morn,
Child's toy,
Mermaid's joy.

How it sings
And offers wings
Unto the bold —
Remembrance
Unto the old.

# Two Squirrels Today

Two squirrels today
In impish play;
Hop and stop
And flippety—flop,
Eavesdrop—and then away.

# Riddles
# for Children

How does a star,
Close or far,
Guide the traveler
Onward?

With its sapphire mark
In velvet dark
It guides the traveler
Onward.

How does a child,
Lonely and wild,
Find his pathway
Homeward?

With love and pain,
Loss and gain,
He finds his pathway
Homeward.

# Portrait

Fragrant, wild,
Misty — soul child,
Soft enchanted flower —
Exist your little hour;
Then as a rose
Age and decompose —
And time devour.

# The Old Place

Breezes veiled in the night
Stir and murmur at the site
Of a lonely place once known
Where fruitful seeds once were sown.
Here is seen now but ruin,
Over all, debris is strewn.
Shattered then, it stoops to sleep;
Covering all, the grass grows tall,
The grass grows deep.

# Autumn Conversation

Leaves whisper in the breeze
An implacable enemy to appease.
Heralds of blood and rust and gold
They murmur of the coming cold;
A rustling rendezvous they keep—
To swelling mound
On gentle ground—
And so to gentle sleep.

# For My Father

He was a man—
Think of him gently;
A dreamer of dreams
A singer of songs
Faded to oblivion.

Say he gained too little
Say he lost too much, —
What does it matter?
Eternity is in his eyes,
Infinity is in his touch.

# Invocation

snow . . .
snow . . .
snow . . .
delicate fragments
of crystalline flow—
bestow . . .
bestow . . .
bestow . . .
quiet peace
on all
below.

# Prophecy
(1954)

The glowing day will blur to a gray,
The spring will creep a hazy way,
The rose will droop without a sun
And petals wither one by one;
The heart within and all desire
Will change to earth untouched by fire, —
And partly wise and partly fool
I shall lament its passing rule.

# Late Spring

Cold
Leaden
Raw
Dark piercing
Heart unfeeling
Unlife —
Then
You
Warm
Shining
Releasing
Sunlight blood
Flowing again
Toward summer.

# Nothing Is Something

Nothing is something
Too cold for burning,
Too gray for tears.
The heart cankering
Sets unchanging
Upon fixed stars.
The spirit yearning,
Inward turning,
Finds no mercies there.

# Dream

When your soft hands
Drew back the night,
I sensed continents—lands
Of ethereal light.
Ah, too strong the bands,
Too late the flight.

# In Passing

It would have been, —
So you said.
But I could not see
Your depth or worth
Nor hear your soft-voiced truth —
For my heart had fed
On lesser things.
Insistent rings
Within my brain
How much made dead
For little gain.

# Two Ages

I watch my infant son in cooing play
As he grasps air and dreams within his fists
And combines these elements with earthly clay
To know of what a universe consists.
His wiser sister fumbles now with light, —
Yet falls from wobbly dreams into the dirt.
She cries to tell me both in joy and fright
My kiss is powerless to ease a hurt.
At some new point of wisdom, praise, or pain,
A place as yet unknown, — perhaps our eyes
May meet and change whatever loss to gain,
A time — suspended moment bridging skies
And valleys — continents of heart and mind;
No more our worlds to search but then to find.

# Omen

Where once a glowing rosebud
And a sweeter lily grew,
A softer, warmer wind I knew.
Now a cold decay lies on the dew
And petals wither in the mud.


# Enigma

What I lost I could not find,
What I found I could not keep;
Ever after—soul and mind,
A terrible harvest did I reap.

# Journey

There is a place I know
Beyond longing and despair.
It's said
The rushing heart beats faster there
And will not go
(Though fed)
But to stiffen and congeal.
Once my love did feel
To lay her head upon my heart—
And was dazed
At how it lurched and stopped and would not start;
She looked amazed
That I still could love
And hope—and live
I smiled and said of course that I did not.

# Regret

A few years
Of often laughter
Often tears,
Yet after —
That point and height
Of youthful then
Never
Quite
Attained again,
Why must beauty
Once we know
Become the duty
Which we owe?

# Renewal

A blade of spring grass
Here in my hand.
O if I could understand
How life can pass
To death
And back again to life and breath—
Had I that power—
The soul that dies
Should once more rise
And live one magic hour.

# For the Future

Let time
And space
Intervene!
Within my rhyme
And in my brain
Your cherished face
And laughing voice
Remain
Ringing clear—
Forever young,
Forever dear.

# Time Was

So soon gone
Is the awaited time.
If with my hand
(Or a miracle wand
  And magician's rhyme)
I could seize the night—
I would force it back
Along the height
Of its ethereal track—
And again await the dawn.

# A Song for David
(1966)

In the spring—in the spring—
What will I sing
As I go to my school?

Of the jewel of the sun
And how growing is fun—

Of the cool of the moon
And the springtime at noon—

O I *will* sing—I *will* sing
As I go to my school!

# To Sandy Far Away
(1967)

When you were five
You knew too much.
Even then
My kiss or touch
Could not soothe your pain
You'd say.
Yesterday
I heard you cry
(And could only guess the reasons why).
O God!
Though I did strive
To ease your heart
So far apart
From me—
My faulty vision could not see
Nor reach encompass half a world.

# Questions

Fatherless child—
What will you do
And where will you go?
Who will reach you—
Who will teach you
What you must know?
Fatherless child—
What would you say
To your young son
Your young one
On such a day?

## To Search

I looked for you—
But you were gone
From everywhere
That once we knew.
Faded now that golden view
Silent now that laughing song—
And I too . . .
And I too.

# Because You Lived

Because you lived
sky blue
was the color
of
my mind
and
grateful
leapt
the waters
of my soul
sweet
was
the wind
and
warm
my vibrant sun
and then they took you . . .

# Wishing

I saw a child's kite
So airy light
Soar and dip upon the air;

I watched that boy and kite
In windy flight—
Till it seemed *you* running there.

# Saturday Afternoon

A grimness no laughter can replace—
A sadness no happiness erase—
Forever gone that glowing child's face!

# A Door There Was

A door there was
Once open
To the size
Of infinity
I've seen
Become a line
In time—
The path
Now angled wide
To eternity.

# Imprisoned Without Bars
(1967)

Imprisoned without bars
So much I love—
And I myself.
An awesome thing
Yet worse to reach
And feel no iron touch;
Across that terrible space
I shout—a whisper
To penetrate those mortared cells.

# To the Future David
(1967)

Dearest son, —
Spirit image of myself —
Unreal
And yet so really
Pulsing
Down the nerve-edge
Time and distance
Of my soul —
I look for you
For you
In every child's face.

# A la Mode

It is hard
To lose the dead
But it is harder yet
To lose the living—
Loving
Rending
Ending
Good-bye now.

# A Poem for David
(1968)

I heard a robin in a tree
Sing a sweet spring song to me;
That pure song which robins sing
Made my heart and spirit wing
And soar in thoughts all sky-blue free,
Of sunny days for you and me.
"The spring is here—
The spring is here—
I went to sleep
In winter deep—
And woke to find it there."

# Bright Vision

Half a moon
An owl tune
Branches bare against the sky
Reflected in the lake nearby—
Moonlight
Starlight
On the winding path that night
We walked and laughed—my son and I—
No wrenching need to say good-bye.
Crickets stirred
Shadows blurred
But our vision seeming clear
As though a thousand stars
Exploded there.

# New Land for Columbus—1971
(An appreciation
from David and his father)

I loved that little pussycat
So very, very much,
I loved to pet that little cat—
He loved to feel my touch.

My little kitten has gone away
So very far from me,
I miss him always night and day—
But that is plain to see.

Somewhere you are my little pet
And there you scamper and play,
Somewhere you love your master yet
Through an eternal sunny day.

# The Way Back

The farm was deserted then—
The fields weed-choked and unsown;
No more the towering green
Of endless rows of corn stalks—
That place of magic walks
Secret and unseen.
Roofless, the silo loomed gaunt and dead, —
Menacing and obscenely red
In the fading sun.
The barn door rasped upon its hinge—
And a forgotten part of me did cringe
To hear the startled wings
Of many things
Beat frightened in the air.
There was but ruin and decay;
Not again would children play
And jump and shout with gleeful sounds
Among the mounds
Of clover-scented hay.
I quickly turned and walked away.

# If the Spring
# Ever Comes

If the spring ever comes
My way again
I will know what to do.
I will laugh—
O I will shout
Just to hear the echo
Of my voice
Against the green and quiet evening—
I will watch the sun
Rise and set—
I will chew a blade of new grass
And taste its sharpness
On my tongue—
I will jump from stone to stone
In gravel-studded brooks
And will not fall
Or if I wish
I may stand and sense
Those rushing waters
Dizzy through my brain—
If the spring ever comes
My way again.

# Years Have Passed
(For David on his twelfth birthday)

Years have passed
Since first I saw
Your face
Still smeared
With the blood
Of your mother's womb—
A sacrifice
Passed over
By the Angel of Death.
I touched your hand
But
You looked past me
With yet unseeing eyes;
Then
They took you
From me.
Years have passed
Since that day
But
Even now
Even yet
I hope for you
To see
Clearly
Among the images
And reflections
Of a new awareness.

# Voyage and Arrival

### I

So often
In those greener days
We played a game;
You'd run
And hide
In
Some secret childplace
And eager wait
With fierce, impatient joy
Until
I would discover you
At last—
Laughing
Quicksilver to embrace.
Tonight
I called your name
And hoped
As in the past
For hidden laughter
To guide me to your place.
There was no answer—
And finally I knew
Your voyage
Was
Beyond my sun
Into another noon.

## II

Bravely
Into the heat
Of that fevered noon—
Scorching
Burning
Embracing
To consume—
Ashes now
That which lived
And green
Forever fled.

# An Ordinary Evening

It
seemed
an ordinary evening
when
my young son
spoke
to me.
I had turned
to look
at
an ordinary scene—
and
when
I turned
back
mind and spirit
grew
so
in him
that
for a moment
his
thought and heart
filled
the void
between us two—
and touched
my soul
and more.

# Memory

Children
Children
Where have you gone?
In the darkness
I pursue
You,
Endless—
Forever—
Never to find
You
Never to know
You
Again
As when
The clock stopped.

# The Attempt

I tried the impossible —
To bridge
The cloudy chasm
Of time and distance —
To defeat
The laws
Of physics and human logic
To preserve
That
Which my soul loved —
And of course
I failed.
And yet . . .

# Choice

When I lost much
I bent to touch
The coldness of the earth;
Life and breath
Dust and death
Between my fingers slipped.
But then a songbird dipped
Its head to sing at me—
And I was content to be.

# For Joe Cameron's Son

Joe Cameron's son
Was
Killed
Last Friday night.
They say he died
Instantly
When
Two tons
Of ravenous
Metal
Clawed him
From his bike—
From dark
To dark
His trip.
"He set great store
By that boy,"
Jerry said.
I heard
Joe wept
Bitterly—
And we
Sympathized
And
Signed a card
And collected money
For a memorial

But
We were glad
It wasn't us.
Well—
At least
Joe
Could cry
And show his grief—
That helps.
To lose
And
Have
To hide your loss
Or have
It thought
To be
Of little consequence
Would be
Just too damn much.

# Metamorphosis

Dead—
Dreams that came
To a child,
Dreams that were wild
And free . . .
Dreams that came
To child and man,
Dreams that covered
A timeless span—
Dead.

# The End
# of the Dream

The end
Of the dream
Too abruptly
Arrived
Would crush
The soul—
But
Finality
Came
To me
In stages
Barely perceptible;
Even so
I wept—
And raged—
And bargained—
It was useless.
I went
Back
To the business
Of my life—
And death.

# Assessment

### I

What is most real?
Is it not most
What we feel?
Yet love or hate in time
And too my rhyme
May fade or die—
Leaving
But that ghost
Pondering,
Wondering,
Ages by.

### II

Who can distinguish
Between the dream
And the reality?
The totality
Of the scheme
Seems merely finality;
At the end
I think most shall tend
Only to relinquish,—
Finally to feel
Only the unreal—
The starched formality.

# Pat's Baby Died

Pat's baby died
And he cried —
And I did too.

Her years were few,
Only three.
How can it be
That we should lay
In earth so still
Who did but play
With childish will
And radiant heart!
So we part.
And I am still alive
Though forty-five —
And so much more.
Did she *know*
How life can go
So soon — before
We see it so?
God!
Pat's baby died
And I cried —
And wondered why not me.

# Lament

Something dies within the heart
And withers in the soul,
And one will search
No more  no more —
And one will search no more.

Something dies within the brain
And cools within the blood,
And one can hope
No more  no more
And one can hope no more.

# Terminal

### I

Surgeon —
Come and exorcise
My soul
With gleaming
Steel —
Cut from my depths
That voracious mouth
Ever gorging
That gnaws
The marrow
Of my being
Unto death

### II

Some wounds
Bleed themselves clean
And somehow heal;
But if that wound
Touch the spirit —
Reach the soul —
There is no cure.
It will fester
Deep within
Until spirit
Soul
Heart and all
Shatter
Suddenly
Into their primeval atoms.

# Retrospect

It fell from flight
But O
That silver bird sang once
Its cool and crystal song
Ere it was silent.

# To Sleep

To be so tired—
I could close
My eyes
And sleep
For twenty centuries
Master
Of so small
Estate
And manor
The while
Humming in my brain
Music
Of celestial spheres
Finally
To know
All
The destiny of men.

# Not a Monument of Stone

Not a monument of stone,
Glistening, cold, and windblown,
But a child's smile —
Shy and guileless.
As for that final word
Set upon the dead,
Take it from that child's heart —
Where the truest words were said.

# More
# Than Thirty

Eternal
One
With the
Rain
Moon
Sun
Stars
Earth
Forever.

# Ending

At the end
All illusion,
Reality fled.
The only reality
Illusion —
Truth
The final
Fallacy.

# Physician

No drug to ease this final pain
Though more potent still your word —
There is no sign today.

# Summer Evening in August

Every sound
Vibrating
With an aching sweetness
A child's laugh
Bubbling
Like clear water
The awesome
Arc
Of sunset
Fading
Shifting focus
The world
Vivid
For a moment
Before
The dark.

# Goodbye Forever

Goodbye forever
Hello at last
The winter storm
Went roaring past
And did what harm
To sing that tune
In sunny June
Was to sever
After
Ever
Bonds
And stocks
And captive locks
To heal
The wound
And hear
The sound
Of clocks rewound
And feel
Music in the air.

# Revelation

The final
Truth
Of it
So simple —
Bare
I learned
Only
As the sun receded
And mists
Swept upon my brain.

# P.S. — And Gladly

You can't
They said.
It's really
Quite ridiculous,
Those peaks and valleys
On our charts
Couldn't be lying—
You must be dying
(Well—You *know* how
Doctors are).
So I asked
The children
What *they* thought—
And
Kara told me
About the springtime
When you're thirteen
And running barefoot in the sun-warmed grass
And Kathy whispered to me
About things flying free,
Stephen smiled—
And Roy—

94

Well—
Roy told us all
About Crazy Willard
(A quite improbable person)
And added some new ideas
About what
A government should be—
And besides
They said—
You can't leave
In the middle of
All this stuff—
And so
I made a pun
And they all groaned—
And we decided
Not to cry
But to smile—
At least
For awhile longer.

# Epilogue

The day is over
The work is done—
All quiet things
Must rest.